The Long Burnout

Christian Kako

Copyright © 2024 by Christian Kako

All rights reserved. No part of this publication may be reproduced or transmitted in any form or by any means, electronic or mechanical, including photocopying, recording or any information storage and retrieval, without the written permission of the publisher. Names, characters, places and incidents are either the product of the author's imagination or used fictitiously, and any resemblance to actual persons living or dead, events or locales is entirely coincidental. All trademarks are properties of their respective owners.

Published by
BookLand Press Inc.
15 Allstate Parkway, Suite 600
Markham, Ontario L3R 5B4
www.booklandpress.com

Printed in Canada

Library and Archives Canada Cataloguing in Publication

Title: The long burnout / Christian Kako.
Names: Kako, Christian, author.
Identifiers: Canadiana (print) 20240433254 | Canadiana (ebook) 2024043336X | ISBN 9781772312409 (softcover) | ISBN 9781772312416 (EPUB)
Subjects: LCGFT: Poetry.
Classification: LCC PS8621.A4647 L655 2024 | DDC C811/.6 — dc23

We acknowledge the support of the Government of Canada through the Canada Book Fund and the support of the Ontario Arts Council, an agency of the Government of Ontario. We also acknowledge the support of the Canada Council for the Arts.

The Long Burnout

Table of Contents

Introduction | 7

The Long-Distance Waters | 8

First Do No *Primum Non* | 15

I Have Seen the Sadness and It Is Us | 26

Cartoon Smile | 35

Fantasias | 41

Targeted by the Rain | 51

"Buber Behind Bars" | 62

Dec. 20, 2021 | 74

Nirvana in Numbers | 84

The Spring Back | 89

For J. | 97

For T. | 98

Epilogue | 99

Introduction

I remember that universe well...
you too, son of my sadness?
maybe you have to age of stone...
sorry for the heart block, I left off the infarct;
too much Holter on the mind still…
nuclear is a setting, should be the final dial.
be sure it was better in the past:
green fields and Smith Falls, parks in memory...
I really love orogeny — particularly when it's on time
imagine, a mountain for a living:
some glacier hip settee, calving ocean overflows...
have I done my part in dusting?
it was pickup or delivery; a doctor chose the former,
it was left untreated, in the end...
I put it all into theory, not practice
I left behind so many words and letters —
make your ways, straws in broom.
do you know if life was really like this?
have you been better at finding out?
just wait till you do your taxes...
you don't know it yet but someday you'll save my life:
it will be in thanks for bringing you here...
but quiet now, universe is sleeping.
hard to make an impression on such a large bed.
would you like to be happy, my dear?
close your eyes, it's Friday:
we can order pizza for dinner.

The Long-Distance Waters

the suite to the next world...
and we're in.
come inside, make beliefs
to be better
move over, Sunday
it's perfect for *ante*
this *per diem* meridiem
for a moon's slot
random pot shot
makes it 13, total
something like Apollos complete
disaster I mean
minus 4 like The Beatles,
just a bit too Saturn V
to be H_2 on the makeshift
bumble view back down
or oxygen blast for a
rocket in reverse... after all,
humans are no dolphins.
planets are no beach.
come home, dear earth...

the sea went out of me
it went in the direction of the ground
floating head down over there
and a drop fall
I could never really follow
with my separation into equals
as it went aquifer where it could...
I went face to face with the pool,
cold chlorine was no surprise
at 9 muscles an hour at most,

yours a type of lung:
prime number starboard breath, knowing
upstream dream, downstream drown—
for a strange exit really, songs already off—
I wonder where the minor keys go
I hear them in every sea, every drop
wherever there is a costar...
behind me is the turn off switch
who could be more wrong?
(the doer of it, the dier of it)
a step by step dismantle the earth,
decrust, falling down aiming
decores this apple
seeing as far as a mountain can
but now send me back to the water
(the closest to me)
water business is never done.
I'm dying all along this diving.
oceans were always ready
for the accidental swim...

it's a virus now, and thank you very much;
break an antibody in case of fire—
stop a coup for the RNA in you
rhyme on the outside, replicant stomps,
ammonite deliveries the sequel,
everyone back to the sea urchins
the dorsal flaps, swimtraps down:
it's all viral and it lives in quiver
it's an under the mouth interpolator
a full-grown adult virion readymade
toxin cocktail mix like Dr. Shipman
it's a dating virus and it's carbon half-life
on a still unsteady earth, wobbly oblate,
everyone under the igneous rock

a collection of identical Nazca lines
that substitutes for other worlds —
and this is the final thought, Ganymede,
on that exit we passed, the resonance
of the last common lung ancestor
the mudfish Lazarus in the book of spike
sitting on desat beeps, and the despair
sticking to 0_2 molecules like dumbbells
sharp edge of a breath is hardly enough,
learning atmosphere as a second language
and still twenty-three more eons to go
hagfish on the next best splice
an all-cop drive through shoot
in roadsign stop motion —
suppose it were possible,
suppose it were infinite even,
all of us junk like our DNA
crashing the Nazaré pandemic waves —
on an amazing new range of glugs
and vocal collapses, convenient set-to's
from zero to 100 bpm and back home again
like stunts on a dead-end street,
a full (oxygen) gas tank on one vowel:
copy and paste it in every cell —
only once that it's daily everything
we'll find we're late again:
always late, late for never again

to complete the coronacene, as studied,
suggest the scopolamine waves of despair —
broken shells and the old miserable selves...
your old crappy identity, tagged up.
you're not there if you're not buried well.
only one lucky one among a billion
will be fossilized in skull and sneer

Elonic of the losers, with cellphone appendage
rediscovered with museum Lucy in the future.
then someone will be famous for 15 million years
and the facemasks will make us a fine layer
between the fission remnants and skeletal remains,
chicken wishbones, plastic forks and straws.
thankfully, the twitteriferous era was brief
medias weren't all meteors and P/T boundaries...
stick it to the virions trillions disposed
pathognomonic cough-coughs in formation,
ritalin movements of continental plates,
we don't need another Himalayan plateau
for our layers of polyvinyl to scoop out,
no Père-Lachaise for our cumulative profiles,
beautiful faces, no botox for the rocks
just chiseled cheeks, filler of calcium carbonate.
we're all for the anxietyhood of humankind,
vultural satisfaction zones moving to the suburbs,
scavengers to gentrify our neighbourhoods
settlers of the west banks crows.
really, it's a dig too far. Look at it.
I propose the comminution factory for later
the zircon layer as jewelry for germs.
the virtual as the dissolution of disease.
and a planet to store everything in
like a big blue kitty litter box.
osteochondromas are in the fossil record
as will be your universal remote controls,
hypodermics, vibrators and pocket rockets,
when the pandemic is finally over
and the placid sediments convolute...
it's cool to be a fossil to come isn't it?

survival as a minimalist
denial as a possibilitist
hypothermia to truth, death by exposure.
I wonder for a long time —
sometimes hold a thought several weeks.
I'm on the surface of a huge graveyard —
you don't know rock bottom
till you're below it, by a mile.
the philosophy of entropism —
it accedes, like statistics —
it has its trillion plus adherents
same lego for all
some sarcasm of metaphysics —
it's present our net worth.
time, the plush for mortality
it comes back implicated
in infiniplicate error code.
some shudders are legitimate,
some just too drawn out.
we must throw ourselves
on the mercy of reality.
looking down on the ground
what do you see there?
a space for you?

look at that sunlight succeed —
everything I never did...
life is hard, and the hardest known —
take it from carbon
just entertainment, for the fungi.
today the cardinal returned,
he stood out, so red in the snow singing;
sounds are just the lookout:
you've been warned of the danger.
I can no longer be the prelude to some

Cretaceous meteor aimlessly lost up there,
aging is all the rage, skin like Galapagos
lumbar like a blue garbage bin
an aortic convention, the subprime index,
proof of existence hard to come by
Planet of the Humans just bum luck
another day painted in fiasco
the light fixtures have moved on
glasses are a success, top of the eyecharts,
so I approach myopia like a challenge
actinic postures and accomplishments,
Pollocks of damaged skin,
the intellectual disadvantage
is suggestive, conceptive;
I mean our whole species is so old —
we've seen it all, pack it in.
time for another day to waste
is that light a tablet, too?
out of the pane, into the pain...

If someone wanted me in another world
could you ever help me there
practicing what I've already forgotten
making everyone believe the lie —
though its atmosphere is never blue
it's an area left alone for others,
a way for uncommon restitution
defined by its absences
mine as by far the most complete.
is there ever help in those places?
I haven't smiled in months —
it's been heavy, it's been hard,
a needle in the world balloon,
programmed hurting, in reruns,
my emotions all dysregular.

I'm known to have made mistakes
I've left things off the earth
(I'll go back there one night)
I've written for another life
I've never been an assumer of secrets.
I've made it all the way through
I don't know how many sad days
and though I left the lights on behind
under cover of night, I lost sight.
I can no longer read, my greatest joy:
I lost the kindness of books...
it's hopeless, it's a sleep too far;
look at those gasps, unreal,
they belong to the bottom of the ocean.
the skies' chest compressions
will not restart my old heartbeat
a world in full reduction presents itself
with help for the white veins,
and they tell me, every day, that
I'm wholly unprepared for flight—
when will I be better?

First Do No Primum Non

the work is just I care for you, nothing more nor less
the head is just the working hypothesis
but the heart works harder, and you had me at history
the ill patient is always impatient
how long does it work to get worse?
those needs to be met, in net effect
and I can't stand long enough bedside up
it must be the worries that hurry them
just wait to improve, do no prove, help up,
and moreover, take no take for granted —
question them, question harm, nocebo
know no evil, lookout, watch for see no evil,
hear it, to do something is too much at times
to do everything is not enough at others:
be careful with that variable resistor dial
everyone like the spreadsheets should be
(don't make that crumpled bed yet)
just more aural meds to mete out among
with the help of an enlarged talking space
like the weather network in the earpiece
the heart on the diaphragm sleeve —
but you were there for me, lubdub,
and for the done what can, man undone
I'll be there for you, in pulse position
hiding behind a whole population now
I make each person heard hard, I try…

you ask from me, perfection —
I don't yet have that.
I have the room for it, the blank form —
but I'm not the way you saw me
comfort of equals to run me through
I'm somebody else entirely —
lost, a bookmark without a book...
I haven't been given my permission
and no one was persuaded —
naturally, I failed the of course —
I mistook you for the good news —
you're asking me for everyone right.
some year will bring an apathy reunion
an aptitude mistook for the concern you had
and I'll take that as an answer...
stumbling over the good enough in reaching
what's never enough for any of you —
angelogy in the bag of practice —
can you cost me more lives
overly journeyed, memristic, holoessential
it's everything think, nothing thought.
maybe I can look it down in those books I read:
there's plenty in the need of shelf,
away and over the keepsakes.
a club of shadows, evening out the errorfree,
carefreely, farewells on the full friends bridge.
some of us are born slowly, some too soon,
guess you could keep me for self once,
and eventually, be the only one...
you ask me to be an angel, but I'm not there yet

there were rumours of a doctor, it was said,
so hard for a smile through all the whispering.
you know that overslough and innuendo,
the kindness of strangers?

no one had it more little known
the hellos that went missing, the good lucks incomplete
and it was so hard to stay quiet
so many were wrongs, and correctly accused:
wrong on the way out, and in.
they're human, I know, like me,
grownups like carrots—
held up for good show, returning early
and they set me up for sorrow
all of it lifelong in that give and take, the equacide—
the work of a survival, unemployed, deficient:
putting me up for adoption in grown age
a way to be wrong, in others, and not myself…

then, somehow,
my empathy dilated grossly, myopathy
to everywhere, like expanding space
a thin layer of pericardium and a lost cause
wrapped up in a da capo arachnoid.
it's torture to undergo the lives of others
they're all substantiated as it is and in full effect
mine in abeyance like tourism
I've given everything away, long before Gates
there's no leftovers, too late for a socialize.
I learned of my soul through distant transmission
I heard it crying once, on the radio, long ago
I followed the trajectory home and couldn't stay.
once, I tuned into emotions, I got stuck.
I worried over the brown dwarfs
and the metabolism of periodic elements,
their hierarchical order, helium to a defensive degree,
the inside out balloon that floats inwards.
make no mistake, on this return trip I would like
to justify the universe to this pain:
a holoform of the losses, accruing…
in the process, I missed out on my own life…

so you ask for perfection, I'll never have.
I'm left in what remains, between the on/off positions
there is no confirmation bias for denials.
the non absolute values, my whole technetium
you want me to believe in you,
here you are, and I'm lost and empty, I'm nowhere
I am not fit for purpose anymore
the grass grew a bit is my idea of positivity
giving myself out, a library book identity
worn out and without a cover
I look for imperfection in sorrows
apologize, profusely, for some sadness or other
performed from the flight manuals of angels
polite of course is solely my purview
only my preposition is not yours—
no, you never need to be good, don't worry:
you were born normal, in the regional dialect…

there are things that are enough
to be once in an infinity:
keeping things to yourself, to no self,
certain poise, the Sagittarius landing,
everything gone for space;
have you been to Plato and back?
a successful mission, unmanned of course…
I must have known myself fall,
I must have aimed to be human too once.
but the book of perfection is hard to close for good:
a few hours each day, show my aorta to the world,
write my own license to explain, feel,
in a burst of creativity, perform a soul,
but poor and imperfect…
at least there's one good consolation:
everywhere in the universe, they speak light…

Doctors are also afflicted with inertia,
like glacial erratics,
a cognizance prepossessed, biases unrealized,
their movements sometimes a little basal ganglial
their chitin in, you know,
cotton white hypochlorite fabric
and the scurrying jointed appendages and eartips—
they never herd together, sometimes never listen,
they too can be riddled with rigor,
or larval, *éclos* in colours,
like Blaise Pascal was so full of coefficients—
man on the stethoscopes, pill on the hammers
it's the conclusion of a doc-post—as in,
the last step perhaps before pathognosis drops
poor agnosis certainly, the ending for nothing.
Prognosis: burnout, slow ash-out,
long embers till December
cartoon heart, helper in the meets;
the window wanderer,
the garbageman year heads up in the murmurs zone
and missing another S4 or atrial gallop
premature death caused by distraction,
a *cri-de-coeur* that never went *chat*--
can you pretend to be a lock when you're open?
charting is heavy lifting, construction work:
look out a pylon falls,
platitudes encounter hope—a love story;
being in series, one after another,
the resistance fully additive...
cold hands, hot heart, you must and you can,
you certified Hippocrates hypocrite—
an actor in the examining room studio—
affliction is a doctor too

Aesculapius my dear in an age of electronic records
time will be your specialist, in the end,
just kiss the kind,
you've been such a good boy so far —

the hospital is just steps across from my house:
they moved some time last week
on the block I live with alarms and monitors all night,
the sterile smell of meds, sanitizers, anaesthesia air
that renders everything fuzzy dice,
I'm left with side effects —
they come in all languages, translating bloating into
various vernaculars
I'm like the zombie hero of Pilgrim's Progress
fighting off lymphoma cells one at a time,
possibly lunging,
exchanging hearts
with porcine values, uncompromising,
prepped for organ rejection
from past experience dating —
inches from my head the iv bag
drips decaffeinated saline
the tick of the clock takes me for tachycardia
I request a sip from the cohabitating
nursing station at 102
but the bedside buzzer shocks me
for missing a fetal deceleration
curfews for C-sections are coming soon
(sure, the mammoths must have suffered too
but now everything is cancelled for the apocalypse)
when I run by it on the way to the bathroom
       I'm shocked
to find the ER empty, no paramedics parachatting

and the operating room has grown grass, Chernobyled —
from Atomgrad with love — it's the ruins of an old
        TB sanitarium
where I grab a ham sandwich on the counter left uneaten
but suddenly from our patio it looks like code black
        was called
it's confusing because I don't know what that is —
perhaps black means asteroid impact like at K-T
but it wasn't in the Kleenex discharge papers;
and I hear fireworks, inappropriately —
is it already Victoria Day?
a mourning dove flies above,
drops its guano in the backyard
as an air ambulance admits another trauma case
        next door
(should've said hi to the neighbour this morning)
I must run out again as a good Samaritan
        in my flip flops,
see if a random ID badge need replacing...
and from my pillow the sirens all sound like hip-hop

I guess I can't handle happiness,
it's too good bye,
& here comes the virtual rain.
it's too good job, quick bite;
can I count by telephones, shut the — up?
a former cartoonist took my name —
made me tame like a cat.
projections of heaven are all wrong
the curve points down now,

these are metaphors all for the same day.
antibodies in the heart, disappointment again
like the Euphrates, my lamescape is better than yours...
you look for your lows — don't hate yourself.
don't haste your own rehability.
ham-mannered, unequal unease,
medicine is the wrong subject
the long-range diagnosis, we all know —
prefer the lowliness, careful for my name.
my achievement in Kelvin, fuzzy information
last year I learned to breathe, this year forgot.
desks for me and chalk for my ideas.
game day, always, for the prospective
helping me to burn out —
forest fires of the unfinished
pardon all my prayers — please, please...

now, after so many years, I find out I am fake
at the crosswalk of reality, stepping on the street
half of me is already run over, at all times
half of me is already the disappeared
how can I be any more inhuman?
only the distance is still left unstepped
there before — I'm left with nothing —
I'm right with nobody —
just the undoctor...
I'm secure in my knowledge of nonbeing
it's still, and it still is.
the last of the sad philosophers,
non-erroneous existentialists.
remember the load of light that was mine
sometimes, from here to Halley,
made up all magnets...

the suicide is exhausted, the paths are closed,
the ropes are all 25 gauge
when I escape the solution
there is the tablet, the 10 commandments:
first and thou shallt not harm...
instead, leave that harm alone...

a pill is all functionless analysis
should I learn from the orexins then?
hiding behind the ID tag of a nameform
turn of the Hymenoptera trade
so what if I'm abused like a sleeping pill?
the client is always right, right?
will a seraph come to save me?
won't a devil do?
help me go back to myself,
there's a return to the request
too many out there to be helped
first do no nothing, no act
where do we see do no harm?
practice the never harm over and over
until I get it right — make it work
make the never happening effective
holster the stetho, make a murmur,
go bland clown and diet advice
first do no nothing, do no promise,
then do no nothing too —
that's the hardest of all.

we humans have been everywhere in the universe
         already
can it be time to early retire now? stay home, downsize?

I'm in so much pain I can hardly think
another day and nothing but blues, tired of holding it off
I feel like a cancer off the nuclear, the utmost gamma,
come carpet bomb some jungle in me
a unique overthrow, suck on the car battery
entire cities disconnect, disturbingly close to death.
stupid aliens, look at the Nazca lines
doesn't it make sense, from the inside it says help!
a career in Fahrenheit, protein farce
wrinkles of an old desert face
inhale the apocalypse fumes
always the product tampering, open bottles of dreams
I'm really feeling the curve of the Milky Way;
it's like the cobbles of the Via Appia
on those overflowing stars, the fountains never stop
and I'm going back to the City of Rome again soon—

can we call it a cure? or just a bargain?
I think when the man is right side up, perhaps.
he's grey, he's balding, he's Leonardobearded
looking for the smiles under the Lisas, like an alias.
oh but I see I have a full head of rain
it's hard to forget it all.
he keeps it all in, like poetry
it's really not a pretty sight;
I feel like my character is all kerning around
a great name, surely, artistic like bread—
fine time for a donut hole right
the conclusion of a Kanner, the murder
of a brain is never a shame.
I don't understand the way time works
there are all the many trips and falls
thanks again to all the profanities out there
a peace treaty with the sand, maybe
we can shift the waters about a bit

maybe to the left of us all...
I want to be, not between
a book for the foot too
step once and for all on this universe
a commercial for all outer space, it seems...

stuff that makes me concerned —
today's mediastinum is the worst, most terrifying
I help everyone every day, I wake up to do it again,
but no one does a thing for me:
doesn't that make my living a lying?
does it make me fake? or just a joke?
and next of course I'll disappear, no one see
no one remark, it's magic hellbent on hidden...
hundreds before me, waiting for the other shoe
ice is known to be the veingiver
the corpuscles that lantern through there
fantastic voyage to the ventricles and bonus a coupon
of another day, another red respiration
hibernation equation, solved.
the catatonic, the well-rehearsed curtain,
the scuba to everyone, of poetic champions declense
and the wellness interventions —
what does it mean to be free?
suddenly the proper noun for death, no longer pronoun,
gender never, prefer not to say, really
look at the pictures of the past, selfies all in thought
remember the pool of the soul?
decay of the weekend, neutron plus positron
scattered in the sky like the colour blue
and it all falls down... look that face in the eye
and tell him you did all you could
you tried all you would
you helped all those you could
but no one could help in return

I Have Seen the Sadness and It Is Us

I stay outside—
outside of the orbit
I stay out of it all
sometimes someone sees me
it must be NGC
it's hard to be alone
like the comet that forgot how to fly
passed the sun, turned back
returned to hydrogen dust
I don't want to be here
there's so little communication channel
my transmission's disallowed
missing mission control
why should they put up with me
but I keep off the grass, sir
well known to miscegenation
racism works with fractions too
no one's pencil more accurate
a modified Galileo in poor standing
so constrained by aeronautics
I'm almost unmeant,
here SETI is pure spoken, no dialect
(—must learn alien languages
google translate "*your saucer's so cool*")
remembering weightlessness on my drive
a meditation rebound effect
don't think too hard out there,
just enough to float by
open house in intergalactic space
foreclosure of cosmos—soon to come
blocktime disillusionment, undertrod,
constraints of the comet Icarus,
his wing waxes poetic—

I'm bad at humans
does the hatred, hate me back,
is it even fair for me to ask?
first law of people: to every I hate you
there is an equal and opposite you hate me
conservation of cool group matter
neosamaritan, can do so wrong
what am I pretending about?
breathing, existing, drinking
does suffering really take two weeks,
double the length of Creation?
dreams go backwards from this point on
exes I saw in my sleep where are you now
date for one last awkward dream
quick rem to remember, then forget—
rush of age, speeding with no ticket,
and no good insights from the retired,
that uni-electoral special interest group
consisting of the have-voted, soon-to-die
recycling with a vengeance of no purpose
putting all their energy and body into compost:
sing the blues of the blue bins.
imagine all the troubles to come:
a world with full on indecency,
no tabs to the sky, flights cancelled,
a paragraph indent for the ground
and for cloud italics, make a new font…
I want to be happy, they won't let me
it's a wiseass habitat, downtown for downers.
I was the smallest person in the world,
for a while in invisible mode:
the magic despair ride man.
loneliness took a long time to learn
and I learned some from others…
did you ever break that bread?
I practiced sadness in my life,

some others helped me with the lessons
what I saw of the rain and more
higher than the long range of terns
when I was right side up in morals
kept me this way forever…
before a life can be saved,
it must be faced
check the turn off to outer space

on how to be a human being —
take good care of that one.
be there a bit.
save the world of grace.
give it up, one fine day.
it's a fake report, essentially,
missing beliefs like a signature
it isn't formal
it's on a paper plate.
on how to be sentient —
you can't be wrong
give forgiveness for us
for me, for you, over and over,
channel the cheek, multiples,
sorry as a motor.
centre for service,
set beliefs in solution
preserve them in pickling —
by your only best standards
let you be known.
say you've saved that many —
old lives coming and going
like trains not all on time,
to holidays, to work, to fouls.
take the messy left soul
with the charge card chip

care of come what may.
survivors, make a break for it.
how to be in the being—
the rest of the human.

they have misused paranoia here:
they're using it to tell the truth.
I know because I fell for it—
they were after me, they backstabbed me
in fact right in the front, told me about it.
they brought in others to do my job, replace me,
and then, told me I was emotionally damaged
which was entirely true since it was they who did it.
yes it's me the predepressed posttraumatic
the one with the radar feelers like a Cecropia moth
furry and fractally branching—
transmissions flickering,
signals that go to identical identities
paltry alter egos that ever falter...
it was never below me to keep my head up
but I helped myself to neocortex
hypothalamic as always, limbic-limber
do you think it's good to be an angel?
today they lost the power of flight, like emus
they remain quite unemotional like snow
white, prostrate like Berninis
kind of like fossils from the old Jurassic.
we like the snow angel shapes—
like butterfly scales—should I still be worried?
is it better to be an enemy, or a coward, tell me?
I will take that other world for granted—
the one without the loss outlet,
the pain market—the predicated cheat,
the nasty bazaar or bazookas souk;
here, the status quo is the Permian

the new Yellowstonian order,
the liquidated tourists of Terra
proximate algae of reconnaissances —
the green men of rays —
unidentified flying subjects of —
& sometimes they even abuse schizophrenia
making it no longer delusion: the voices I hear
telling me I should be dead,
they're telling me the truth…

I know catatonia so well
once a month turn my head like the katydid did
my compound eye has so many settings
not every blade of grass is locust stuff
immobility works for a living
a crust of mud at the corner of the eye
where the sleep gets thick like Miami beach
I know alone so well, better than I know myself
ego hard carapace, an exoskeleton in DSM
I'm all the best proof that excess poetry
can lead to a heavy burden of mental illness
like Kilroy on the white walls of the ward
thoughts are everything I container
constant brain activity is the scalloped
pilgrimage road to San Melancholia
(*Do you know the way to Sad Jose?*)
I'm so good for death, but so afraid of it
everything a mess in the weather concerns
downstream from the sky and the upper-dromes,
terrible are the times when words won't help
though silence is no better, it builds and kills…

meantime, in the American Heritage Dictionary,
the news is bad: populations go missing,
it's everyone for themselves, we copy diseases by hand
from the stone age to the meme age, backwards it goes
everyone willing to see merely realizes
it will only get worse for all of us
even numbers are contrarian as hell
feeling the need to count more zero…

a moment of silence for a moment of kindness
every time I drive back from work I realize
humans are autosurvivalist motogrades,
they turn on the cognition in a cardboard box head
that mostly malfunctions, like car alarms —
let's be aware of the losses here too
losses to come, losses to be, neglected losses;
though a philosophical injection to the deltoid
would never help *les autres* — so reluctant
to lift the muscle of an arm or thought in aid —
remember the pathways to the lost addresses
returning to your circles like a target shot
the bully's bullseye again, flies-lords camp streets
you're going to be a record too one day
the black flat kind spinning at 33 $^{1/3}$
when you're run over by winter tires, Method morgue,
as the spit from the area codes flies like rain —
and what has happinessed to you far from
that music? as a witness without vision —
put the graffito in Plato's cave: Kako was here
a lookout for the milky way spiral arm one
a starfish on the wish, inside-out,
constellation minus, a moment in the centrifugal turns
angular business of all needles,
is it a sleeveless heart on the last stop?

just a fugue of the next move—
habits of patterns running, falling,
the time is never now, you can see it,
the throughput is the Constantinople
slow progress happens within, without...
you were kicked out of Marcus' Meditations:
you wonder how long the life goes,
the river rows, bucketseats of the maps pass,
and you have been in this lifespan before
(no danger to others when alone)
they made you move on, they cut everyone off,
tailgated and ranted, so let there be from now
flags at half mast for all our half-heartedness;
let's stop at all our exits to remember
for all people, for all freeways
for all highway culverts to come and still to be:
a moment of silence for the kind words passed away...

come with me to nowhere, happy for the ride—
blank blank blank
with nothing left to say
looking for the sheets-hearts lie
it's exhausting to be real
I can't speak for myself—
I am the closer flatness
I am the midnight I made each night
getting up Jesuit, helping me pack
the overnight intergalactic trip
coming home craftlagged
with nothing to say, nothing to do.
Sundays are the hypothesis
null: nulled, nulling it over...
my paper spaceships fly far
the looseleaf drive in a rocket font
folds of the letter *b*...

a salt in the brain and no taste
compendium no exit, no entry
joins up with the space markers —
imagine them there —
& I'm on the flagpole.
shake the heart, man falls out…

who could play me in the remake?
poet escaped from the terrarium
maybe the only one with no firsthand knowledge
of having once existed here, a priori life,
a pro at recumbent despair
a hospitalist as a true fugitive
the quicksandman for freestyle, from a deep dive
to take a piss on the red carpet
the boozing bozo, balloon of enzymes,
the collection of the infundibulum
ricocheted from birth off the maternity ward wall
to a stage by the light of the retina
with the upper eyelids on tape delay
returning for an encore to project his voice
to see and be seen, for once visible
scrapping the eulogy for a made in China fake.
it's so complicated to be the finished one
both original and first off,
directing a script from memory remotely
and then the specters of spectators
who might hold the applause too tight,
futile playback, written without record,
a fully ironic Telecaster
played louder than anyone could ever hear —
at least there's space in the radiation still
rectifying the wave equations of sources,
out there, everything is balanced:
they'll send a cosmic ray upon request, or

a complete set of the works of god.
and then who, indeed?
the real estate agent of sadness,
the mortgage that had no number.
an illusion of first principles,
a consortium of the breeze cappella
a sparrow with a completely new song.

OK now exit the best planet.

Cartoon Smile

remember poetry is poverty without the v sign
so what am I waiting for, room?
someone took a star out today, left me at home...
I'm stuck again in Plato's cave
(think Nebuchadnezzar II by Blake)
thinking of the total losses of rhyme
demonstrable patterns to rocket exhausts
space capsules to bring us back home;
poetry is the longest part of language, no?
sorry—longest lasting figment of nil,
I meant to say, Rhapsody in Death,
Le Sacre du Mort… in time,
we disintegrated, detrited,
it was successful, many people died
as said the revelations in the end;
today it's *yolo*, and *fomood*:
fear of missing out on doomsday…
the pavement has a way about it,
and once I walked out of the dictionary
(as it all started over): *I love poetry,*
but the suffering is sure hard to take

it's ironic to be me, it will be
even more ironic to have been me,
like an unsettled score between body and soul
a tiebreaker to last all time—
Jesuit in status epilepticus—
help me work off the resurrection
lose a few extra pounds of dramaturgy
it's another form of anaesthesia
yet unknown to medicine: the stay at tomb kind.
to keep it off the books for later.

a shock can come by email, nowadays,
a life-changing effect of profound suddenness
of great importance to sadness, like my father.
and in my life I never had the opportunity
to be unironic, except perhaps as a baby.
though I had an alibi at the delivery
I knew ambiguity, ironifluous on or after birthdays,
now as an adult in appearance
so much is more realistic than I thought
sunrise is cathedral, you know
lives are for real if they're someone else
(except our daughter, who never made it out)
people will never make sacrifices for me
I was never worth it for them, ironically
maybe not even for myself can it be done.
with a left-handed brace for the heart,
perhaps functional for a week, by force
can I help them like they never helped me?
such a team of unproblematic illiberals
as straightforward as functioning appliances
who never saw the inside of a poem
big black dodge ram trucks for intellect
abstaining from abstraction like cinder blocks
now as I age, what befits my identity
is the constant irony to not be me—
you're lucky you're exactly that, and I'm not—
late night sarcasm, standup conic,
they mention it always in silence,
for I only have myself to hide
to have written this and to have read it,
as an application of the real Socratic method
to constant critical disregard: blame myself
for not having been, in the future
blame myself for no longer being, but only in the past,

and in the meantime help me present myself
to be on time for this flight delay —
put myself in my own shoes that don't fit

I never found a language that worked for me
a dropped sound would make me miss it wholly
then a mouth would move, I'd be startled and be gone...
today I only ask to be healed for good:
I need to be sure of the word for peace,
to hear it when it's still in the air —
but in all those cost-effective metaphysics, nothing...
others found it so practical for one another
homework for signs to be, the hands Athens
or the telekinesis of a smile sincerely yours,
an oral curl chorus, some current state for application —
a whole Florida to geograph, for example
and they're right to be kind with it, well they should be,
all around the hydrants, neighbourhood sir tories
languaging for hours, with enough room for parentheses,
dependents, subclauses, couples of footnote:
grammar is drama, happening aside
as I bewilder the news, disappointed on schedule,
an asterisk who left his nouns in the rain,
library groundhog with no shadow,
for me, in unsaleable syllable, it was never there,
words didn't put out or post-it for me...
and think of all the other creatures that stand down:
a humpback whale's song can travel a thousand miles
his cry for help could cross the entire Atlantic
(and therefore come too late)...

you tried me out and I never heard you —
the loneliness is never wrong, is it?

and I just found out, the word I is already taken...

I remember how the insulin mattered —
it hydrogened in the burnout
Turing the lights out
stepped into peace, like a circle, pi vs.
poetry, the cost to eternity.
oh breathing tube anthem
the words that matter, hard to rate
and a minute dose too
committee for suicide, arbitrage
you want to avoid that sunny day nightmare
it is not interested in scientific truth trading —
trash talking the theories, you know,
meeting with yourself and its minutes
is it the final clause to put down?
tomorrow is in multiples of
as always, on the paper airplane wings
of philosophy, nothing gets cut right
size it out, sound it out
who gets to take the origin point?
who gets the z axis?
smarter than the truth you might be
with exceptional teraflops, a gigamonster —
but intelligence is still the cyanosis...
Beyond the Valley of the Sciences
will always be there — appealing Apollo...

say you work the letters, one at a time —
you occasionally make meaning —
unfortunately, some you base your life on.
you slip on them like sunk stones.
treacherous, as they say, like the cliche.
I need the yellow vest too to write
so they'll see me before they run me over…
have you crossed the Milky Way already?
one more time orbital, functional analysis.

they make you sleep like squid
and now keep you liquid... solvency,
it's the oneness.
spirit of every close assist;
the chi, for another game it's
the statistical ghost, interstitial souls.
some things you only remember in the abstract.
definitely not pain though,
nor those eyebrows.
sudden illusions, and the sad looking afters.
a record water fall.
how do you justify yourself?

I can't believe my words sometimes
do I make up my own existence?
just for one more page?
there's so much pain in the world already—
how can I possibly add to it?
In the Annals of Internal Suffering
everything together in one parable now:
embryonic nothingness—the movie.
in the birth registry toes to come
fingers cowried into fists, limpeted
it's been helping to lift itself up
not even a hundred mothers would do.
reaching for another story further on
in a poor impression of verisimilitude
he crawls, an undone hurry.
the cell divisions, the decisions.
crux of the crab art,
the box office calculation—
he covers the waterfront stars.
around the Lindberg crossing
it matters on the phytochemical return
the last pocket for the eyes

absolute haddock opposite lookdown.
god was set theory, axioms,
all the way to the end —
zero o'clock happens now
you sleep you lose:
the book of Genesis
never really got going.

over the poet, there is noise...
jet engine reunions, air marriages —
high altitude clouds with heads in cubicles —
but they just can't stand the sadness in his eyes...
it doesn't matter, he can't hear anything
a blocked intake in the wrong manifold.
the weather forecast repaired, for now,
he's cognizant of the flight risk of the wind
he's on the unnamed path of the wrong map
delivered to the locked door of escape
so you can't talk over the silence...
line by line, he goes gradually missing:
English is a backwards pedaling chain;
he tries so far to be conclusive
but when the hum comes, it's absolute
whoever's closest to waking spells it out:
he shall be reincarnated as a whoosh.
somewhere a schizophrenic assumes his ego,
continues the calls of tinnitus...
so far on the planet, it's been ok:
for the cabbage white butterflies it's ongoing
great box office smash on the big bang
but magnetic tape is our sustenance
on the world that garbage is fated for —
as extreme quiet carves out a slow orbit
by sound waves with nothing more to say
Mach one is subtracted to zero and they find
the most unlikely spot — for his metaphor.

Fantasias

the time machine works both ways:
it takes you out of happiness
and it takes you out of pain
is it ever really worth the ride?
you know your way around there,
don't you — didn't you —
the distances so well preserved
miles of the squared cubits
the lucks and it sucks to love
unpredictable except that end.
the sun never wonders aloud:
never about craters, about Venus
about the burning off of oceans
about going red giant tomorrow —
consuming the earth in fire —
the extreme happiness one day,
suffering in the next transit
the switch sometimes broken
clicking in the off position
the height of the crib once
a core that never solidifies
back and forth breaker interruptions.
are you helping yourself
stepping inside the reaction chamber
sealed and sound-proofed
happy in the morning, sad by noon
desolation of knowing no travel possible
to the many restricted zones
making everything out of old circuits
repossessed from old appliances
shattered glass everywhere,
steps on the infirmities

and the metallurgy of despair
the contingencies of yesterdays
and surprise deaths, next chapter over:
is it all really worth it?

we're the best in the world at finding nothing
it's been so distant, like a radio antenna
with an articular surface to the earth.
there in the darkness, it's easy to hide
but we don't give space a damn either:
the pi of dismissal, ready on time,
around like a loop closing in.
it's another lost equation, exponential
but reserved for some more unknowns.
with the most sensitive detectors in the world
the most expensive systems ever crafted
we have the technology, we've got to find some,
and once we do we've got to find more:
we know there's so much more out there.
I mean it's probably everything, isn't it?
because there's no dial tone, no line signal:
no indication of anything, anywhere:
at least, that nothing is coming on time.
transmission in a point, with no dimension.
self-talk with hypocrisy, irony, selfie-stick,
self-absorption, the electrocute complex
and in the first person, anthropomorphic we.
telepathy can work sometimes down here,
although it's not quite error free.
we know it's a dream world really
it smells of consciousness and it stinks
to whoever has a normal nose to fall on.
we're so far into the future we're lost
half of us with acquired ADHD
the other half with acute loss of directionality.

all so nuclear now, this one big family.
one Pripyat to rule them all
uninhabitable thousands of years yet.
coremaster, in an entire buried switch.
flexion is a spectrum and so is kneeling.
electromagnetic took up prayer as we asked.
think about the beams that left us nothing,
the gods that gave away everything,
they created for days, for no one.
they created for nothing,
Chariots of the Gones.
I guess rewilding the Milky Way
does make a lot of sense.

in the dream equation there is no equal sign, is there?
no sign of minus either, not on this page.
there is no return for the dividing line
no mark of infinity, for killers like Cain
nothing to say we're in control
not even a lock for love.
there is no solution for the differentials.
a budget dream, an infinitesimal heart:
no more than a soap bubble.
a tattoo might be seen in the dark
like all the stars that went entropy before
because the skin is individual, distinct,
correct in its concealing, as always…
for physicists there is no dream theory
quanta of nothingness make up all
into the bay, a final peace
on the sails of the aorta.
there is no equals here to sign…
by day, the lotus is my symbol:
it keeps its head above the fraction line,
cup of white for the reflection of light.

(For all the Conspiracy Theorists)

father of the flat-earthers was round, wide and round—
and he appeared on the big screen so large—
he stood on the Great Wall as seen from space
projected his thoughts, diluvial *a deux,*
knee deep in sea level sang the hallucination anthem
nominated himself for every folie
which was his follower at held heel
with the third dimension an unplanned reentry
burning up on the altitude map
from the dot product of the vector field
cummerbund of the latitudes in the most formal
mercatorial equators, him and Pangaea
governing tradewinds, on the holographic principle
he said, take your cosmological fighting positions
be flat in affect, like the galaxy Andromeda
father rpm in the 78 vinyl perfect pitch
tin pan alley to the spheres, Charleston turn,
flat like time you don't spend as the father
that flunked the volume, cubed, on the speaker dial
flat river, flat driver, and laid ocean
though even his birthday cake had layers—
had and ate them too, not liking the icing enough.
he denied global warming, in this case
cast a flatiron pan in the flash
and never made it to the tip of the ecliptics
like Antarctica, hottest property market around,
from the conic sections of the conehead
the winner of Atlas Mr. Universe in contest
Greek superhero of the supercontinents
laid down in the lowlands the lowlife geeks and
the flatbed monster trucks on their mad runs
Pied Piper, he meditate levitated Himalayans to crash
on the flatscreen TV for the next Netflix doc;
he was canonized, lionized, unmasked, antivaxxed,

laminated, succumbed to the voices to be deified
rotating around the axis I, axis II
PD of schizoid like the discoid orbis
circus maximus for all *morituri* he showed
the taller they are the harder they fall
off the sharp edge of the protoplanetary disc...
now message delivered, post goes poles
and there couldn't be a better coda:
because father the flattener levelled our earth...

did you ever hear: they dressed up all in
lab coat-bleached white for *les 400-coups*
    whooping cranes:
costumes with long beaks, with black stilt legs,
    with wings,
used trampolines then pommel horses
for their chicks to help learn
to fly then perform gymnastics,
later flew man-sized gliders as guides
and finally, silicone-valley-generated rockets to show
    them higher up—
It's true. At first, they used forceps for grubs 'n'
    worms to pinch
what's snack up for their fledglings' long
    chopsticked beaks
before, when their parents mated, an egg a year,
    humans would whoop!
and help with animated pictures, VR technology,
    sprayed pheromones
in front of romantic sunsets & cinema backdrops on
    the sound stages
they rented from Universal Studios, played back their
    most accurate
reproductive mating calls tuned to perfect pitch—
they had to separate the pecking orders into cubicles

so no one ever got hurt,
they used swarms of CGI holographics
for the mating competitions
and omega'ed the alpha males;
hired contractors to make nests of the best twigs
    twined for
IVF eggs hand-picked, hand-delivered, nestled in our
    babies' cribs
with congratulations signs in cardboard cutouts of
human infants set on lawns
and they had to bodyguard the young'uns, imprinted
    them with
secret service robotic adult avians five feet tall,
taller than any other robot species, levered legs
    remote-controlled,
then they used flamingos painted in Penaten-white
emancipated from zoos, Audobon employees
    contractual with
their pensions in shrimp farms, trained twenty-year old
    swans on stilts
with baguette bread crumbs to usher them out, and then
they took back from museums
and first nations headdresses
the long black wingtip flight feathers the birds
    had been missing,
still authoritative with the immensity of their prior
    inhabitations;
and over all their ancestral feeding rest stops
they blew up parking lots to make stray marshes
wrapped with swamps and wading waters for wet
    invertebrates,
(making them undrainable by laying concrete yards
    underground)
they bulldozed housing subdivisions and projects
replaced them with well-stocked fertile ponds
    full of shiners,

the batrachians, the anurans, the salamanders never
        before seen
in suburbia, they curved the East Coast of the United
        States on the topside
to make it a little easier to roadtrip the troposphere
they heightened Van Allen to signal South to their
        ocular cytochromes
who had never even seen Atlanta, Georgia, before,
in the process they made Aurora Borealis a massive
        green sky vision
that made the whole night an emerald green theatre
        closing curtain
then, still to help their journey,
they reseeded the whole of the
Northern Hemisphere with old-growth forest
and wilderness,
for extra continent, added another new
        Gondwanaland of beauty
and, in the end, they created a whole new Earth—
that had no humans beings on it anymore.

'the Dalai Lama urged researchers to accelerate the path to
transcendence so he could spend less time meditating — '

so they built for him a superhighway,
with eightfold paths,
and he made his approach to the speed of enlightenment
where time slowed close to eternity like consciousness
but he got stopped for a moving traffic violation
when he turned the wheel of suffering too fast
and he was asked to contemplate the consequences
none of which he had faced before,
by denial of self, denial of self-involvement
guilty of complete and pure innocence,
then the negligence of identity accelerated

the right conduct sped up, he was forced to conclude
the total of all energy in the universe equals zero
the condition of rest is the infinity of velocity...
but the laws of motion were everywhere,
and later came the converts, the pilgrims and acolytes
from the ads for abnegations, the commercial Zen,
the enthused, the bare-haired women in yoga
ordering samsara to go in the drive-through express lines
and it became over-crowded with rushing onlookers —
an elbow disconnect, a dry movement of droplet vowels
continuing the wrong conversations of complaints
the cursory meanings of life, incarnations...
they gave it away for free, like Costco
the two for one deal for nirvana nonmembers,
nothing could be seen from the conglomerations
though they were organized, they were impatient,
linearly disposed for so long, promised absences,
in a spoor of colourful clothes and sweat
following the riverbed to sediments;
they ruckused and slammed and caused a traffic jam
just to the northeast of the state of samsara (posted
on Instagram)
and everyone was slowed to a crawl
and after an eternity they stopped, with time dilation
just between understanding and forgiveness
in a dilemma of confused denial, self-negatives —
breathing in and out slowly just like before
the same as when there was nobody at all
until the exhalations stopped...
so at the first sign of nirvana we all fold

and when did the Buddha ever face a lineup?

why so glum, tardigrade?
solar storms are refreshing
nuclear blasts are a blast
you winter round the stars
with mushrooms for the tasting
gamma-radiate your all-star tan—
so much space to slow walk
ride up on a pink helium balloon—
float for your ticker-tape returns
last I heard you migrated to Saturn
stowaway on a NASA payload
where we met helium on the wing
laughing gas of the gas giants
carrousel of the pebbled rings
rode around the extinction crises
scaled down the Kelvin return
hydrogen helper for lunch
zero is a comfortable temperature
absolute everything like vodka
too much news is detrimental
it's no longer entertainment
perfect time for doomsdays
earth's wars are opportunities
all-star survivor, all-planet player,
no two-way ticket remains there
it's plain sailing, endless summer
here in the upper holocaust museum
don't be sad, wipe your eyes
waterbear in water-bearer Aquarius

are you a god?
do you hurt the ones you love?
do you break things fast?
would you like to make a lot
just sitting at home?

are you also engineered
for obsolescence in a year?
you don't know how the feelings lie—
you're naive, like a sea urchin
you're empty now,
like the Big Dipper
you're tungsten with no flame
you're always missing the last page
so the epilogue never ends
a gross interference
in the great plans we all made—
Hell is no place to hide—
no more universes for you…

Targeted by the Rain

I see happiness as a distant shore
I'm swimming and I'm tired, but the water is so cold
the temptation to give up is so strong—
why do you try to be such a tough guy?
I don't—just no one asks me how I am
there's a difference, being quiet for the good of
humankind—and letting all the waters go free—
who is the maker? who is the father here?
not me, this child from another two strangers,
product of another figmentary egg.
to be responsible for the wrong is the hardest
the mistakes that make me heartbroken,
the people who suffered from my fault...
dreams entertain with paranoia-puzzles
calculus masters of overdrive,
exams that were always there to fail
the blank page is harder than Apollo
the moon doesn't have a lot to say.
a trappist heart, impenetrable landing,
I learned it well and I see it often
it's like, there's no underworld to it
a middle-class application is what I'm in
topographics to the inevitable
like infinity, something never realized:
the geological age of sadness—

nothing to say, and more so soon—
said with so much atheism.
orthonuclear is the arrangement of atoms.
bilateral symmetry makes everything simplistic
and this premature spring with war starting:
what was it that died today?
that lovely sound, it was as if we never cried.
the nuclear weapon is evolution's best:
genetic power in full completion.
we failed in the passage of time
it was a lifetime of bodies at rest, really...
a sad comfort of medication will be needed soon,
don't drink yourself to sleep, company rogers,
the solvent that dilutes ventricular csf
is the part of blood that isn't red
dreams on the outside looking in
age in salts suspension, particulate matters,
tourism on the cosines of snoring...
the waking moment is strategic, Bismarckian
hallucinations all work together.
everything point form and it's wrong
well considered inferiority complex
wet hands of kilogram pray for the nailed
a hieroglyph passes through a synapse
it's a pyramidal tract and it's pharaonic.
thoughts are closest to the truth when wrong,
we must suppose; we can use them still
as a suspension of belief, a bridge of hope:
don't be so sure of our own inevitable passing

death is the division of two irrationals
one Chinese in the style of kingdoms, the other
never-ending in the manner of $\sqrt{2}$.
no hoarding these doomsdays
drop it, leave the world off this mess
trapped in space on all sides

a page of words, a waste of time:
in times of peace you talk apocalypse,
in times of war you call your mom,
that's how we are
you can't do much with poetry.
good lines rarely come up these days
and in the morning they're all forgotten.
such a big mouth, so much gets lost in there.
don't believe in luck,
believe in that of others close to you
it's an explanation for all the call waiting:
to be always left hanging in the end.
remember how far we are from space
as if there was too much night
and gravity's upside down.

we had so many earths to waste at one time:
it was so long ago it was like a dream...

a broken man, in pieces everywhere
under the snow, under the pool cover...
be careful, the word death is particular
it requires judicious handling —
it's a bit too definite, too totalitarian
in a heart of heaviest lawrencium,
radioactive to the ones nearby.
the disgust existence, like it's always been —
pertains to the universal emotion —
how, how could I be me here?
how could anyone advance such a futile cause?
all these broken lines, and a broken life
footprints of syllables on total loneliness
is it you that thinks this is me?
who are you if I think it's you?
the fully furnished thinker, sitting on a rock,

like Alcatraz, poetry of meninge
and it's all happening in my absence
the ground sliding back into the ocean
the oceans evaporating into the solar system
the universe expanding with more emptiness...
I saw those places return to us
and once I reverse engineered outer space.
far in the Dirtyverse, the defunct and gone
days of the last decades.
from now on I'll never move.

that light may as well not be here
it's useless, it always misses
it spends its time loitering, in this room,
over on the other side of vision;
a window breaks it open, like Easter
it hits my closed eyes offside
penalty against the science of physics
it's as fast as anything can be
nothing can exceed it or its miss
its essence is photogenic survival from
eight minutes of a boredroom meeting
it emanates from explosive rage
it's hated us since Prometheus
it brings patterns that don't follow
a record of my face in wavelets
gemming the surface of that pool
it insists on carrying on, despite the cosmos
it's a lapsus lingae, set unprismatic
in Salt Lake Mormon vault again
the always-time-for-more resurrection
that switches to Stonehenge standard time
as the present can never stay,
trapped, at a summer impasse,

alone fork for the missed shot
for the light that made an own goal
you may as well be an identical photon:
it has no exact existence, spread so thin
it has no place here, doesn't belong.
& I've made mistakes of the shadow

despair is a planet
it orbits so far from the sun.
I am inconspicuous of sadness
I am a broken hand in prayer.
I am the habit of the leftover,
just hanging to the bone.
unhappiness has built my home
nowhere else I've ever known.
doors open to the inside,
people are never late to leave
no welcome is overstayed, ever.
apply to be shell and
wake up to the wrong day again.
your life is mine for a minute
it wears me down like back pain
I can never be a patient
you complain about me,
I can't complain about you
nobody made those sticks too thin.
malpractice makes perfect.
then, hopeful way back to a cure,
later to be a hanger-on
sublimated closed space
the gas phase of the room.
I laid off the life today —
out of a big pool of dreams
I took out one of the last.

do you know those holes in the ground,
they're everywhere.
a sarcophagus was found under Notre-Dame,
it was once used in another temple.
I never know where I'm going, when I'm back
I wasn't told about how the soul works
it was considerate enough being born
making a clean break of the waters,
but even the children can make me sad now
they gave me 15 years of happiness and that's it
now magically, I make enemies of strangers
I make strangers of friends
fission can be with neutrons of soul
sometimes they make it so high in the sky
sometimes they go so far in the ground
to this day, the inner workings a trade secret...
look at it — a storm of no one
a locus of facultative anaerobic, to be seen
breathing like a whale and
learning to hate boats for a century
the wars that will soon presume us there
we've returned to vegetable matters
do I cover the air, keep it tarped,
performing arrangements of Mach 1
for shoulder shrug marathons again?
the total weight of sadness on this world
must be heavier than the planet itself.
look out for the jetstream, and its translations...
how to be alone in zero easy steps.

now it's time to be lithified
as happens to wood
for each of us there's a bird somewhere
a needle of compass in its bright eyes
constellation calligraphy is their calling

magnetite is their migratory
they are bound to leave by instinct.
I've heard about the lying rock there's gossip
the impression is a solid like a trapezoid.
a cell is a stalactite start
it's able to be calcareous and stratified
and beginning by bone, build up granite
by enamel and alphabetic vitamin
take a seat to a new sediment,
continue to continent
rearrange the elements to spell your name
periodically reappear on the surface.
to be patient and kind, you can be shiny
smooth and even difficult to move:
to be heavy is an admirable quality.
orogeny is destiny
they massage in the uplifting,
vacation in Mica.
Carrara is a wonderful career,
limestones sometimes higher than towers
they flitter like the Sphinx, sometimes
a whole Cheops is apical like lungs
captured Thebesian, a scientist in Mykonos —
a pillow for your bedrock.

how do you hide from the tears?
they leak out to maximum visibility
an exalted supermarket of salt
with deposits that dried up in flats
inflationary like bryozoa, recidivists,
they soak into everything,
they stain like laundry...
alone is a roadsign, a face card
you must count slowly
when you count down from one:

sudden death will be a big surprise
save tragedies for plays,
save comedies for adieus
all the same words will surface again
with liquid paper for embalming fluid
make it to the next clock and back
every quotidian shelter cuts minutes
you don't need parking tags anymore—
still in the market for loss of sadness?
can it be given for a Triassic smile?
never forget the children
who sometimes make it out alive
they concerned us all until they left.
keep faith in the forgetting
in the absorption lines of tissues—
open the tear, it's reentry for all salt:
you lost that game of life to others
you never really knew the rules

an extreme example of existence—
on the way back down to normal
as you pass the others, step by step
show some slack at the last one
an island is enough for us lizards
slipping it all under the tongue
six suicide attempts, at least one successful
and you're still going strong
it takes your breath away
Clytemnestra is a byword for the borderlines
you'll smell it from the antagonists on up
the Jesus theatre plays well
psychosis is the generic name,
schizophrenia the brand.
it's so useful in constellation.
you know it's the jerkwater that tastes it

colas start a revolution, happy up
and coma down, neuro-infinities again,
it's the last place on earth
they know how well they'll end
in a bucket like crabs at the beach
in the -ation ending with no noun
in the elevator brain, emergency stop.
it's the head death comin' on thru —
awareness is a rolled up welcome mat
the inconsequential -istentialist of the ordinary.
exit exist, even Heaven can be Hell
not knowing the cosmology of this place—

superexistentialism—it's the usual you.
but death is our right isn't it
it's first in the bill of rights,
it's the last amendment, ever
it's the million light years backwards
survival—the remake. The philosopher, stoned.
it's happening on the edge of the universe—
flat-earthers are right to say that cosmos is flat
(consult with god, the fellow of the royal college)
it's feather-likely to be you, but higher dimensional
reality in the time of Fermat solved,
the classification of nonAbelian groups done
it doesn't happen everywhere at once
it's like the theory of tectonics in identity,
a rock like the candy, sucrose dissolution
if and when the logic gates close
as collateral the heritable universe
has said it all, it's you and it's done
it was a wave and it crashed:
wrap up the life, oh saran

happiness is so imprecise in its aim,
it missed me by an entire planet
though I'm only a short drive away
coming up as a stowaway here
I wish I could hide from everyone
throwing away some of my old stories
I have nothing but sadness for you,
man without a sound of his own
I can hear the surfaces reflecting
errors of everyday genetic replications
hurried to the wrong exit, obliquity forewarned
I've always been a stranger here
just keep me afloat on the smallest hope—
I'm weaker than the floor of the cloud
where the rain falls through—
a placeholder, convenient for the identity
invites me to the last chorus:
now write down one more line here—
right here; practice it, excel at it,
say it, then, go ---- yourself…

Hello death, is it me that you want?
I'm here, I'm waiting, always waiting.
I don't leave where I am, I'm here still
I was here all along, just passing the time,
no need to look for me anywhere else
same home, same marriage,
there's only one global positioning coordinate
silence is the last call
moving to the next satellite observation
bring your own nights, I guess
deal with it, afternoon
one local movement I make in answer
in the practice of the heart
with the backwards stethoscope,

what the murmur hears
you might have told me the length of the trip
and I must have known how old I was
I'm finished what I had to be
I'm bored like you, I'm undercomposed
no one wants to save me, coupon unredeemed
chaplains have been worn out by me
the hedges are all untrimmed
the crimes are all unsolved,
oh yes it's 24 Obverse Place, here
nothing good is ever said,
even in secret, in silence;
what those weapons are for —
only the silence is aware.
go, close the sleep too.

"Buber Behind Bars"

I hate it when the medications don't work
the room stays eightwise cornered,
conniving via closed entrances,
words evaporate or are transpired
messages never arrive...
conic sections of a soul;
best fit on the plane its tough ecliptics...
our days are still numbered, recursively,
computers crash with aplomb
the mind is distal to the foot
it's every protozoon for theirself
asexual reproduction screws up
summer butterflies post no arrivals
heart's transmission breaks, gears lock
DNA is recopied dysfunctional
the transposons all go nuts—
it's see no madness, hear no madness
as the psychiatrist always speaks—
those derivatives of the unknowns
x, y, and z receive all errors,
3 am is still my workday
faced with EHR hourly horror
scheduler the agenda orange
this is the barcode, self-checkout
Form 1 for all your needs—and then—
waves of pain, pools of sadness...

inside the pill it must be round too
—something like surround sound for light—
but with little to hold on to, to grip,
a hand will be teleology, middle Devonian,
cluster sensation at the rim, unbounded,
more individualized than could be practiced—
you slip, both forwards and reverse symmetrically
an ankle beneficial to the possible fall—
a virtuoso cadenza whole rest measure
& there's barely enough air for one
there's never enough silence for two to share
parrot *non loquitur*, speaks for itself—
it might be green, like the earth in reverse,
a snowflake of its own design,
the Sea of Tranquility at high water level—
an area over the head, and it's safe
it's not careful, it has enclosure, posited,
it's a curved play, both coming and going
both touchdown and launchpad
an analytical requiem, polytonal,
like the imaginary numbers that dance
and stay calculated for your grave—
it's a mistake to not be nonplussed,
perturbable, phlegmatic like humour,
here imprecision is the way to proceed:
doubts travel the universe now
the neurology of Cubism is apparent in windows
full degrees of freedom in the arrows of time
the space redaction for an unmanned crew
antigravity freefall, spit up the Coca-Cola;
and round water means a new planet
habitable like a homeless shelter, doesn't it?

all around the test station from Soyuz
past robot Drosophila, shooting past Voyager
where Venus took the tab by surprise
when it flew too close to the sun
and melted its wings and fell, it's circular,
it's circumferential, it's curved, it's orbital,
it's π times something; it's radial…

then finally there came a drug that worked for me —
but it only helped for a moment of truth.
a momentary death.
fate was way too fast.
wasn't fair,
wasn't too easy either
in fact — all those preliminary results,
they didn't pan out — I flunked…
destiny situations that unlasted
overwrote the overridden…
too much to be, too much to see —
generations have passed
since the last big solar low.
a Maunder minimum misses us.
sunspots now are nuts,
it's like, e equals mc 500;
gravity ain't nuttin' but a number —
a score to tell the dose
tell it for the index fingertip,
little braille-boy-blues.
it feels so good in the crumbs
nitrile, latex, slap on the wrist,
in times of plenty of poetry
many tried, many tired.
like the blue crab of tabs,
an all-American,
just some washed up on
the beach of beer cans

and I'm a pharmacist too,
I work the back catalogue, like old Sears-Roebuck
I make pity out of milligrams,
drama out of disbelief suspensions,
I don't do over the doses.
it's normal in the morning because
I've been left off the earth too
it turns, in a way, without my bed
a complete circuit in the core, or partway for me.
they have been numerous when they died:
tomes upon tombstones.
remove the appendix and then continue,
remove more, progressively passing outwards—
and I forgot, I was in the Bible too once long ago
as one of the loaves in the fishes
they make miracles of wicker
and I turned it into lost slogans on a roadtrip.
I've run up an outstanding bill in the ozonosphere
closer to space, flatter than the radio frequencies
I'm a rubbernecker in a scattershot crib
home in the comforter, the severe, terminal pillowcase
not even anymore a wannabe alcoholic;
I'm not right in any angle sense, in any hand I have,
I'm not justified in any formatting
and the time to put in all those zeros
like the binary code octopus,
we count them still in multiples of *damns*
sometimes in the filings of iron,
in the magnetics of migration.
mortality is always on those comeback tours—
I recommend the last to die, go first
add water to powder imagination, then drown.
the parabolic is shoulder to us all
and the death lock drive, the racing hearts,
the crash-the-cart curve make up the
thickest ghost in a long while

I'm a defeatist in times to come
I'm a hard man to be wrong on.
this down is the softest
this year has been the hardest
it's the fleece, the feathered flight,
and hope? nope…
the all-on contraceptive action on me,
neverending rain for the uplifts
and once, the time machine shot my mother
so then, I've never been born, again and
again and again

different meds, different days...
the life of a poet, always in need,
empty spaces, so full of volume
enormous needs, so drained with emptiness —
in my twenty-fifth year the quintic equation
insoluble like the age of Cardano
was a due date in the past
the proboscis as a senior manager
different dreams, different monotony,
the language at the tip of the space capsule
(type of thing) these are dissonant harmonics
the demographics of drugstores remains
the lives you take are only one but
I'll take two of those, thanks
nothing is more Zeno than this —
sure, The Ace of Deaths is the best bet.
do you want to talk Prospero?
born from the sea, see what it means
he has a prescription staff too now
going into those many ATMs down
waterproof to all the heavy dreams…
vacuity of nothing in my empty —
the 'depth of my longing' it is
to circle those tablets, like the drain

look at the pool of the pill, so round and blue!
was it the last reaction of that sun above—
set it in those warm water excipients—
it so speaks in the diatonic scale, sounds to love
space that's fresh being all you need
the waves converse in secret messages
going to the most beautiful, begging her to stay
are those reflections the most favourable ones?
does the rainbow cut corners too?
do you go start at the deep end, where the
cervical can be reinstated as congruent?
the curve of this dive is rectilinear too
—hold the air to the side, we don't need it—
this might be all the fabrics of Ophelia here
that might be some of the new water rhymes
they license all these waves to come and go
opening new passages for hurricanes to pass
always on the blue side of the eyes...
on top of the blues of things...
the diving in, and then the drowning out—

have you heard of the last pill?
it goes into a hole in your head
it takes place like a cinema surround Dolby
it escapes the pulse and really gets lost
like you do, you should
nothing but articles of disappointment to draw up
and to pretend it's useful for something
like an accessory ear, supernumerary nipple,
a necklace worn on the inside....
warm on the outside,
I will cite my sources to the soul
the work of references in the head
see what the sky makes of these senses
sometimes the garbage trucks in formation...
oh look at that again—

son of the pinhole camera, sets
an eclipse in Orion as I said
meet me halfway between those irides
where grace meets for example
a plane in the throat,
take place in the breakfast, altogether now
room to grow
to absorb and be gone—
definitely, for all of you—
I heard of a head that was made that way.
good and bad in equal proportions
Tethys at a time,
Pacific *alles in ordnung*
to whom do you owe allegiance?
if you love this planet, not to them.
three strikes of sleep, in a batters cage.
let's not be hierarchical
the plan supply company,
-azepam the saviour: somewhere
it's all happiness and light

I took the medication—what more do you want?
to shut the f— up? to feel an effect?
Fall of the House of Ego
generations are missing in action
people lose on a two-cell-stage dime
places for so many decimals, unused.
why was I the one, mother?
take me back, country roads.
they come from the disconsolate outer reaches
two fingers that grip like an OK sign,
the powder is the dust, still.
the sun is an incident, I suppose,
a drama of upheld dreams, and it sucks.
same day is gone for everyone.

I call on it to remain unremembered:
it was worse than the one before.
a happiness entirely at the wrong exit:
highway stars, night maps, planet signs,
sacrifice of the self in times of plenty
turn back, make the illegal U-turn...
I am the last dead end, am I —
can I never shorten the hour
dismiss the longest heart;
as I slowly walk away,
suffering longness of breath,
so happy to have one day off, from me.

today I fought the pill, and he prevailed again —
do you have someone who loves you?
everything can be lost, it seems.
I made my promises too narrow and small
and now they left me without evidence.
I was never a member here.
category zero error — it's a mystery.
but no one can win philosophy
like a video game beat the big boss.
unless, save those suicides for another:
they come back, at 3 AM,
faster than Plath, curt like Cobain,
a dolphin for each ride.
oh to be the alcohol of a parent —
did you help me make it to the shore?
a message in a bottle: Leffe was it?
did you lie to me in it, on the tides,
was there no translation for it?
a cup half empty, half shattered,
tailgated by those bolides,
movements of glass in the symphonic
adagio in the tropics of anaerobic

one day put your footprint in the sand
on a beach somewhere, stay forever,
not like the last time.

everything I can see from inside the capsule
upon the topmost shelf, F-16 fighter model.
a hand drawing of my father.
a ticket to the inverse of me
the person I will never be.
a corroborative exoneration
in the blankness of their faces.
odd is the number of my cells I count.
the sun on my bedside,
look closely at its milligrams
warm in the toe of sand.
this is the expansion of the universe:
one day, two pills, three times,
and it's a chain reaction;
the unstoned life not worth living.
silence so full of our music
through a full diastasis world.
the domain called obliteration.
a calm in the wrong galaxy.
a roof on the other head now.
everything except a way out.
two yards to the left of the eye,
and a magic brow reminder.
...another lost heart in space...

within the dream it's all dark now
measuring diameters by feeling for it
I just want to be alone
infinity is on the way to work
how can hope be such a grand finale?
it's a sharp edge to reality

for all intents and purposes, death—
a holdout for the keepsakes to come—
my fatigue its own foreign language.
why is it always me, come home from broken heart?
it's the everlasting Jennifer
the hotel full of vacancies here.
dreaming of a smile I never saw.
alone is the hardest census.
flood of the eyes, ark iris
was brown, wasn't it?

the sedative makes you silent
just sad enough to be conscious.
the heart printer squeaks, out of toner
I'll put my things in order
slippers by the patio door, loafers in shoebags,
my books fully chronological and
check bank balances in the middle of the night.
pay the bills tomorrow, rest up a bit.
'when you thank the pills,
and they kind of understand.'
someone loses his veins
blot blue in the albumen skies
a bridge to the bed, lost in consciousness.
perdurable conceptions, looking for identity
in its mathematical oneness,
the universe lost in space translations,
micromanaging creation in
hopeless engagements with the
sensors of reality.
but wait, it gets better:
there's absolute silence in space too.

do you see the stars out there?
they shut them off for me.

at night they take turns lying to me—
resting, you see, in the way of all milk—
asking me things I don't want to hear:
have you seen the supposed soul?
do you know the repository of vision?
even the comets ignore me
passing me by without turning,
their faces to outer space, and
I'm just waiting for this day to end...
the nights of meteors falling down,
of moths flittering up to lights
no one can see is all I've known,
look at the way I make shadows only
in principle now; I feel nothingness,
it's pure like xenon, complete like lead
everything just wants to add sadness:
is all that weight not enough already?
it's the nothing that makes me whole
the crosses that cross my paths—
the need that I am empty with—
—the nothing that I am filled with—

the pain comes back, it suffocates,
it sits on me like geology.
it storms me like Jupiter, it red gasses.
one day, it'll aim for the monoxides.
straddling like strangler fig roots, it *macht frei*.
it breaks every skull in my body.
it stands ankles like foldout chairs.
it helps my lungs to the flight zones
it makes my heart serve carbon well.
I step on the stones of tablets to drown,
a new commandment says do not live.
I go backwards in evolution
pre-Chordata, to the aqueous phase.

I'm the serial killer of nihilists,
a serial suicide of existentialists,
the wrists of the last species.
do you bikini atoll yourself?
thermonuclear is a really bad day
hydrogen bomb is its married name
with some radiation sickness in the way.
from the Nevada test site to here
a flash was a burn, a lead casing,
a heavy metal meant seriously,
Geiger it out to infinity.
take it—now double it.
the actinides are all inside
gamma the matter to the last bet...
it was a desert already wasn't it...
it made that granite mask, cold on the cheeks.
they make saints out of marble, you know.

'let there be dark ages' he said
'let them be long,
let them be very dark
let them be shadowless,
insufficient, togetherless—completely—'
and indeed they were.
there was no communication
there was no sound for any words
there was no light, no source of light
nothing to see with any light,
nothing to be or to become.
nothing once was.

they are there now.
they are nothing.
and at that time silence again
completely filled space

Dec. 20, 2021
(Rock Bottom and Below)

I had a dream it was Christmas
and everyone heard it sing
the lights stayed bright
there were no bills to pay
there were no reasons to leave
winter was a tasting
considerate with snow
up in our living room
blue compounded more sky
sunrise came as a marionette
there were no taxes due
bureaucracies made no fuss
people never yelled
lost friends smiled again
and no one left us alone
on the day my father died…

1.

news of death is never overdue
a snowstorm can't escape it
it's the layers that just make it colder.
overall, the emphasis is on depths:
reductions, residuals, the executors of god's will—
it only happens to everyone,
but it's helpful if it's always put off.
there was so much to read about:
the chronic renal failure to die from
to understand it not from the sidelines
but from the actual playing field, doing it,
killing time those final months...

like a father to son short circuit—
solder burned off dreams, tomorrow for no hope
oh god, do you remember where the lives all are?
stay of emergency, so often a lie.
catastrophes can only be postponed,
complications make the sky.
the winter solstice, uncooperative,
was so everlasting this year:
a chronic *minimum extremis*...
firefighting is another outcome of hell,
and the world outside a travel day
pretending everything normal…
but this is a problematic Christmas season:
a death all on the wrong holiday.

2.

the break in the heart is long and narrow
it's the wish, and the disappearance
it's looking for either lift or off.
the cliff, the rocks, or the dive.
through the window, outside, a concern,
an area that supports light.
the rift valley is considered irreversible too
bones poke holes in theories there
and in the Red Sea, it's see no evil
boats and beliefs, Ararat of ark...
to disperse the claims of real irrelevance
get stoned, make a mark, a bridge to the letter b;
pandemic is our punishment, our flood
all these waves and the mega hardships
the mergers in tragedy drama
break sadness like bread every day:
cold home, for living stones
moving to the bedroom at sunset.

all our spaceships are like insects now.
everything enters in one split split—first or second—
the division chamber, straight and thin—
and narrow, like a crack—intravenous thought,
put it all in underwater saline, one litre drip.
my father smiled as he lay dying...
the old stoic made up his mind to be trusted.
I remember some parts of the Pentateuch well.

3.

father on the death certificate will stay
time on my mind will delay.
I'm starting over; help me to crawl again
lots of ground for the newborn snow
and in the distance the blindness rules
it's just to land on four feet
regulation fridge, regulation nothing
there are three friends to my name, none extant
concave like Plato, last a little longer
a little byproduct, the inner condensation
just entropy now, all of it thermodynamic
like peace, like nothing.
if everyone forgot all numbers
we could be a baby or old
a paper cut for an existence
first a birth and then a grief
from the maternity ward off evil
no alarms for birth, no reruns for pregnancy
no numbers, to look from high.
another cosmos away, look at your name
in typographical rectitude.
do you know the last father was here—
is this the meaning of a child?
the wind can be a minister too...

what the apostles once called work,
legitimate least squares it is,
to persist on the pronoun until 3 AM —
who wants that resurrection, anyways?
it's a clawback and it hurts, no way
to stay patient with impatient Time.
at least he knew it, the old man:
that trees are the delimiters —
that Decembers are no hearsay —
take guidance from the geese
no way that god is a poet
never was, never will be…

4.

I wonder where the good days go:
a cough in the next room
jaws that crack in the night
a scallop for the ways to be
all my expressions for area
over, forwards to the past now
it's something like tragedy again
the expressions of help go wrong way
I have a sleeping pill to my name
many nights of sweats to come
I have an octopus for a stomach
I have a language all of never
abandon me to the orphanages
when will the spring be standard time?
it's pain, from the bottom on up,
from the conscious on down, and
still all the covid customers coming by…
just like that, notes for mortality.
be quiet, don't want to disturb the suffering…

children there, like the word always,
singing; but in the pointing away....
far away, like the look in my eyes:
'daddy, why do you look so sad?'
time is never in band arrangements
and the collective pillow, a sack alone—
there's such a mystery to the pain.
an innocence, in the guilt of it.
two children, two hands, mirrors
to what I've seen and been,
a lock of compassion, an inner secret;
they're so much deeper than oceans:
I hope there'll be enough dreams for you
you gather gold for hopes, shells for help
you dig so deep for answers—
I promise I'll be happy again someday.
cross my fingers, hope to die.
good may my luck be.

5.

to test myself to be there—
am I alone, am I not home
am I still here, like he is not—
compared to the air, everywhere
and I'll be just along
a mark on the right page
a correction to be known
it's an unknown in the face
a tear in the right bucket
a birthday not in effect
they passed and they moved on
no footnotes on the way
are there those who never made it
fails of another certainty

fact of unaffordable truths,
fools insufficient for us all
arguably, the paper, the verso
perishable properties have been forgotten
a percentage was left behind
over there the list gets longer,
the message is what's done
and every death counts, doesn't it

6.

catching death, like a cold —
return body, hopelessly locked to the wrong side,
where do we try to sleep, at night
they are turned, to the bedside
the head always on a pillow, hair there
brief scent spot of your shampoo
patient like ladybugs, where
windows support sills of light, sometimes
and the pain too is a rocketship
packed bags with powdered foods
one day, the fatigue will take over the universe
for grief, in addition to high viscosity,
is slippery, it comes before
as well as after all the big deaths —
dreams of a final theory —
sons of nothing take part in games still
exercises that resemble the equalities
the short story comes out of life —
maybe next earth I'll be better?
the last delivery of stars —
greetings from another part of the solar system.
the sudden area of visual curvature,
Freddie the sedative never lasts long
and I'll be done in a bit.

I'll wish for that happiness equation:
Einstein put it on the blackboard,
then forgot it, absent-minded,
the numbers went higher than infinity
they sang till the fadeout of the soul
a door, for light, & envy is blue—
Death, Poetry, Taxes—
now mark and honour past joy
like an anniversary day.
and that was the day I became old.

7.

but you try to hide, the grief finds you
it lunges about your burrow
like the heron that swallows whole...
better this, than the other...
protractor lies to stay in bed.
the man who fell in all oceans.
lung formality, to persist respiring.
it's just an everyday pandemic now,
high up in the virus.
landmark illegibility, unconcern,
rest will never be in peace.
mental awkward, no basic science.
tedious dismay, lost flexure.
it grabs you, wherever you conceal,
in the clinic, in your hermitcrab shell
it sniffs you out in the bed.
there are holes in every room.
humans beings that go particular.
properties of declensions.
an arrow in the back like Otzi
the iceman goeth, groundhogs down
like glaciers ice shelf off

Patagonia of the cold cheek.
already by noon there's neverending...
but the grief goes farther:
in the distance looks like low clouds.
you tried for a while at life—
mother was the way out.
now tear your eyes out like Oedipus.
you be the ray of darkness
extending outwards into the cosmos.
an urn is a valuable, to keepsake
from now on, as long as you can.

go, someday, in a day all of dreams—
curtains for your part, and your whole.
don't wait for the sunset, it finds you.

* * *

there is like a clay of Pompeii here:
the dust so close to the face.
I cover the area from death to the ground
and below, I can see it go
I know the sleeping will well
I own the floor from the feet on down
I'm there, I'm there, call on me.
a mountain on my neck,
can I do it with consistency.
a century has gone missing
pyramids are the masters.
my father died on the winter solstice.
I went back to work the next day
but it was really hard…
a life is just sunken costs, right,
all of it cognitive dissonance.
I'm leaving it all behind...
all the thoughts I've heard before.

there are no messages from outer space today
there is no life on my planet.
there is no *how are you* here now.
just oceans that are missing areas...

I asked for completion in the planets—
now it's done, and it's just so.
eight for another go.
it's the absolute zero of the heart
black and gravity and all that falling:
everything lost in the one direction...
lights go on and on in this universe
but never shine on someone:
depression collimator beam.
I make up matters with a breath;
sad map places me next to those
emptied of time outer reaches,
universe inactive again,
all unnecessary cosmology.
people go so far in me,
everyone an astronaut now.
the earth is down there, tidally tunicked,
most popular place for most:
it's programmed to save lives, you know.
and the dreamset theory, so circular,
so able, so fantastical in despair—
leaves me at nothing left to say...
too many times, I've belonged in landings
through an orbit never even fixed
with this planet so supposed:
its restrictions, places in surroundings,
lost parameters here and there,
the vacuum insufficient—blue baby,
born for freedom, bored for free.
reentry is a burn kind of lark...

Impossibilities matter —
they matter in millenia,
they matter in me.
a desert is a likely location
vacuum makes the universe.
manger star goes missing
harbingering no birth.
whatever returns to never,
must belong to never.
mechanical time, for the time being
lift it up on cinderblocks
clock strikes zero
reflection of a light means no
but I'm still conditionally here —
this winter means I surrendered
a failure in the meaning of madly
pocket of air remains by the couch
impossibles abound, crowding out actuals
was it me, it wasn't you...
left of me, the wrong side.
millenia come and go,
no love matters.
illusions are always placed
in strategic locations

Nirvana in Numbers

the robber was the Buddha
the eightfold path was an ambush.
it was too dark in the elbow of the temple.
just as a straight line can't exist
a road can't be turned like a page.
I gave it away as I had to, and I lost it all —
I must've breathed in the wrong way
and I missed the air.

he took the hope that wasn't gone
he remembered the life I'd once had
in principle, he never strayed, he just hid.
he said wrong way, it's this way to happiness:
misdirection is the signpost of narrow paths
exiguity is the perhaps achieve
to fast you must be too slow.
everything I did, in the end turned out wrong.

he's the best at surprise perhaps,
a jump out into the oneness of all,
toad pond in a ripple, wave swim to the centre
looking for a surface that doesn't end
following in the drowning points
that intersect with held chests.
it's the middle because it's the deepest
across it come all accidents.
the splash is the uncovering of water
without the sound, it's not wet,
a pool of water from which to remove thirst
when the animals find it first.
it's the lotus that led me astray
it's the light that went the wrong way.
without asking or saying, for a long time I gave up.

would I stop talking about myself
would I have nothing left like before,
would I stop eating, or achieving, or speaking,
using words that have nothing in them
when I spilled them like water.

in the place of tears he left a seed
that absorbed all its moisture.
in the place of ground there was salt
and nothing grew.
so hurt on the many paths in —
where to go to, to be lost?
it was 'run philosophy' directionless
it was the last come first.
it was being in the least heartbeat.
it was beating in the last heart—

he took me for a victim,
he took me for a fool.
the Buddha was that thief,
the eightfold path was an ambush...

to breathe at depth,
to find for me an older ocean...

plug all those meditation leaks
make sure they never make it out of your head.
ill-advised it is of the ionosphere
to subject us to its philosophical insulation
too often, the breathing out is retroactive
and life is never an unconditional thing—
carbon dioxide is an entry point to the future
it sweeps us up, it means us gone
there was a living past once, like the memory of a story
already over, you should've breathed in,

long and hard, like a cloudshaped sigh—
it's an age of Advil Liqui-Gels and it hurts.
and what have we done with the thoughts
flying overhead like passenger planes?
they multiply in the vacuum, they stick it to the stars
all the places where the heart leaks too
like the logarithm of a lifetime
by a disorder of magnitude, in rate of change.
the sound of speed varies on this planet
it varies on the modular frequency too
where your breath once fell, you'll say
this is where you left it,
when you should have corked and kept it
when you should have made it whole.
watch, that meditation makes a crash landing again...

and can you really meditate yourself to eternity?
it's such a long way to go you know
breathing out, and the atoms wind up everywhere
an increase in air pressure through the galaxy
even life says nothing about this
small animals are the last to bring it up
they are never so involved in ahimsa
it's understandable to be impatient with endlessness
it's the hardest thing ever to not attention deficit on
the mind returns to domestic chores
like a dishwasher running out of soap
perhaps that long yawn was a masterpiece of
        transcendence
it gets ever closer to an open mouth
a cartesian near term birth can be satisfactory
overall it's original to not be in dog form
go back to the plane of the intersectional lungs
can you really coordinate all of geometry too?

maybe you misplaced it, a rotation too far —
here and there a star comes out
a setting on the slowest turn

back then, nirvana was a number.
back then it was an actionable result.
now, it leaves everything out.
it's a tab on the left that you never use.
space leaks in from the vacuum outside
it's like desire in reverse
it's like a person you have to ghost —
you have to activate the pumps to keep it out
it's a big part of existence now.
you need enough universe to last a lifetime
another round of breathing all round
keep it up for another night
all good people, stay close
but you wish for the lost quantity....
it's an unknown, perfectly round, now gone
like the girl you lost again and again.
meditation happens only once a lifespan...
and life — do you know how it works?
the unborn are made of this
you shower with the materialism —
clean with currency, speak with metabolism,
alive in the planet earth's saliva
along with all the others...
look it up in nirvana for dummies.
software engineers, back it up
before it crashes, again

In the Pali Canon it is now day:
the sun is multiples from the mountains down.
Should we close the book of the night now?

there's enough of its strict decoherence
there are two tomorrows in every direction
there is one sun behind and one ahead.
I remembered you, could you remember me
I made the meal I said I would —
I put it down and I never ate it — I just waited —
did you?

This river, it runs wrong.
All flow is suffering.
There is everything in my past, to come.
From the setting sun down my neck
the fold is in the hand, the palm, inside,
so follow it closed to the end —
there have been promises before —
in the turning cyclical
there have been thoughts here before,
they were accomplished by even less
this, by the thousandth birthday
you will be delivered again
to bear the good for the proof.
Have you done well enough to be still alive?
there's nothing good or bad but it will end.

Carelessly, I have hurt the living
and I have suffered,
I have heard the living never give back...

Bodhisattva, let me be here one more time
for one more sunrise —
this time, the next time, for real...

The Spring Back
(*For my Family*)

it was so sunny today — funny,
there wasn't even one sunbeam for me
they fell all around like a house of glass
they fell at a glance.
did you corner the last Caravaggio
it was David on a plate, and Herculean
metastable that is, in phase
on another island where it was so sand...
sometimes Poseidon complains
now everyone thinks like a figment
calculates like a fraction
a modern denominator, low galore
common in the Piscean paints
the suns never add up.
colours are off, the additive UV,
D, barely dines gallons
who did I hurt to get this way?
I've rolled out a few portholes,
window warmer sundials
around the angles of now, but
some Sundays come with detractors,
so open to a dash of sun's ray:
sunbeam me up, Scotty,
we're through

unexpectedly finding a lost dream
complete with closed captions,
it's on the shortlist for a prize, of course:
but my son took up magic with the sunrise
and it helped me to stay...

I wrote a book that no one read, once again
you might have found it in the dark
bumped into it and put it back
all about the sadness and its plant life
a catalogue survey and quite in depth.
it was a hit in triplicate for the flying cranes,
200 more than they parted, left for nothing,
back when no one went more interisland...
wintertime was to poetry as
understanding was to abeyance;
I had a cramp in the afterword
from the last bad stretch and yawn.
for years I followed a handheld way to frown
I was a Sagittarius for just one star
the binaries went back to their places
shaking their coronas in sad carrousel
as all the good hearts were spoken for
then, to my surprise, the sadness came back,
and this time, seemed to stay for good
I hit rock bottom and found a way under —
I wanted it all to disappear —

but my son learned magic one day
and that was enough.

(Victoria Day Derecho, May 2022)

I could barely hear myself cry over the rain
and when it stopped our tree had fallen,
smashing our entire backyard...
you couldn't leave a forest alone?
(I'm nsftw: not suitable for this world)
some trunks and thoughts go deep, still fail
on the ground such stubby obstacles
their bark Dürers etch for bare zygomatic arches

their crumpled leaves now green garbage
their timbers were flying buttresses once
scaffolded for polished marble to climb up on
their roots were our supportive care:
off it goes, another good neighbour left our block
now conservative lawnsigns are everywhere
a democrat comes last, climate hopes crash...
a tree in the shape of a skeletal quadruped —
consterning not just to the arborists I suppose but
a splinter in the township's fingertip,
lightning made visible in chiaroscuro
Brownian stillness in fractal constraints
sharp parts, so hard in F sharp, common time.
a lake is made in the mind, hillocks separate
water collects there as a remainder after division
I come closer to drowning in there and
I come closer to being downed too:
it's only one tree, only one me.
If I stop writing now, it will have been enough —
but why is the language so unworth it?

do we know how the spring really works?
take it apart but it comes back together.
you don't bend it far enough, do you?
some songbirds can, they use magnets
to curve the earth like Columbus.
ferrous filings too can line you up
Van Allen in the fast lane
bud in, get kicked out, make it up
at the cinema there, hook up,
bag of popcorn, palm of grains.
field feed the plenty, furious Foucault,
pendulum for the asterisms
high for Deneb, Altair, and Vega,
return is irremediable now

go for the *v*, with your misnamed *w*
white letters from a featherpal
plant a seed from the sky scale
an oxygen valve speaks volumes
for any old respire repair:
litres are indicated for this.
take the baby outdoors, moms,
smell the air, fleet, commune, clip
bouncy — slack the hydraulics —
this atmosphere is free of corners —
it's not just some other hypotenuse
putting in the least effort, to succeed.
no one makes it work:
pays its crummy salary.

in a technical paper, the happiness was constructive
with a Mercury arc-seconds movement
all on the advice of quartz, care of daylight savings bank;
though I didn't think my conclusion was likely:
the backyard on the other side of the fence green —
and myself the neighbour over there,
with upside-smile, turning down the squiggly face
loosening the vice on the jaw-wrench
monkey-man of the trees, rebrancher on a
goated scape-human, come out of nowhere guy:
a hominid fossil in your rosebed —
I can always do a better job of being kind —
they tell me it's free, take what you want from me —
I can be the man I always thought I was,
in brown cardboard and pop up card ideas
up to his eyeballs now in blue paper layers
for the good of the many who never come.
May 29th and it's happiness out of season:
for the unbelievers who debit the sedimentary rocks,

the sensate gravediggers, for Hindi in prose,
all the Sanskrit that was sent, I vote
for the long way home (with eternity to come)
so breathe and consider it done

it's a spring if it's here
otherwise, it's a lie — a big box hoax
like an Ikea down comforter, just up,
bumper sun, calmer for another oxytocin.
spring has always been another language
the mother tongue, hitchy hill
like the red wheel barrow in minus 1 sentence
the farthest woman, the longest hair,
new days bubble up better
I'm green like antennaed grasshopper
size XL of day is everything
noon is for the index finger
the sky supply just footnote,
and knees for the warmth —
longing for the good ship mitochondria
slip into portside broach for
as many fleas spring, as may fly in

today I fought the pill, and I won.
post hic, ergo propter hocked and ever after
postmodern euphoric irony,
the heaven ice cream truck ringing its bell
and an arcuate star of forgiveness:
do you know your happiness from your well,
your good enough? collect all the seeds...
so they triage trees now:
I hope they saved some lives today.
the pool water is perfect,
the phylogeny is pluperfect, it's on asked

a common cabbage white kibbutzes
and I've made my own way through
the self-atheism, admirable, admissible:
no self-miracles, no self-prayers
but after this, and not because of this,
causes go farther than ever now,
conservation of good, like energy, like momentum,
is allowed to be allowed — as well.
the bed of flowers without rest
it's the understory of the forest
plot complications second floor and up
this instant is a coffee without a cup
does the loneliness stay in intergalactic space now?
does a living once, figure for reward?
days on end I did it, letters to Provence...

and it's pollen day too
you were backwards, so snorkel
as if the water was just a toe
as if the waves were never repeating...
circumstances of loaves,
just enough to be you.
there are tears on the leaves too,
people cry for all kinds of unreasons.
you never forget a mistake you made.
we never learn the speed of sound.
I've taken you out of the echo...
I think we know it:
you hurt yourself on a year up
though you grew connected like roots
never like nitrogen fixation happy.
the dandelion seeds, they're all from you.
they use our children to propagate.
(I gave you too much of myself,
I'm sorry... say it's OK... may I
see you say it one day...)

the sun is on my side now...
it's ovarian, take a deep breath,
it's OK to be happy
it's OK to turn mediocre
to decline in colour and taste,
just once is often enough
it won't be unforgotten,
Mr. Parkinson will not intrude.
senses and a half,
chemical is the light of this
Maxwell's max wellness
gift in terpenes, I swam laps
of lapsus linguae
I tumbled to the bottom, at ease,
harnesses of shouldered blame
breathstroke again in viable
flipper to forelimb, finned to finish...
spectrum blue, I love you,
sometimes don't even need poetry.
those who are dead are forgiven all
they fail to elicit further embarrassment,
such lucky ones...

so one day I said, the sun is done
one day I did it, I turned it down.
on a variable dimmer switch
I made it fall.
shooting pens into stars
just doesn't work…

it's OK to be happy, you told me
you can be that much the less for nothing
for an entire universe, you've this much space
there are longitudes within you
lines from the script that never cross
just a girl you never saw
and the dreams, they go on for miles too

an actor can achieve great acclaim
as someone else entirely, a happy man
with very little else aside
and so can I, unnamed in fame
in units of minutes that flicker,
I can be the doctor of brain-example
I can be subsonic through the happyverse
calorific like the plate settings of sun,
a thermostat to keep on its toes,
soul-conditioned and so cool
to be out of the forest for good
to be positive like an algebraic unknown
at a crackdown on the repression of goodness
and a concerted compassion will assist me —
sometimes, on earth, there are periods or commas
for the locals to gather and group, subset,
so belonging calms go on for long
and an occasional kind moment takes me farther
it's derived from plants, it's unsaturated
it has a lot of healthy fibre, so slowchew
people who didn't care of course counted most
for them I saw the world for what it's worth
but now it would be helpful to be happy
an agenda for Dalais all over
no benefit of a doubt...

it's OK to be OK again, you said
just not yourself
on an ill-considered century
paid on a sliding scale of selfishness
you troubled me to be here,
a father who made me cry —
now the darkness has wings to fly

For J.

I had the sun in my eyes
and I had to turn away
it was too flight that day & blue
and the city itself was the star
wider than Betelgeuse ever was
copters made round territories
a downlongtown in the smog—
exit past the sage brush no. 1
you remove yourself by dates
sunlights the show, it's fatidic
so much for the pink air,
the sheersome surprise, the royal road
Daytonic in driving back
pursing burning in the epidermis,
the collector tan for all time—
off the observatory for angels
a monarch told me to stay,
to look up at the stark contrast:
of stars lit up by haloed streetlamps,
of freeways turning off to outer space,
of deserts and mountains altoed
for your unachievable height
I love you like good luck
I love your beautiful bird
long down feathers of your eyes:
dreams always screenplay the future

For T.

how close are we to happiness?
daddy, are we there yet?
what is the state of the mandate
can it be visible upon approach
though covered in fog, concealed by rainbow
so far off the odometer —
over by the breeze, a waft of butterflies
they have contrails in colour —
of the carbon romantic, you know it's said
standard issue sky jacked up and such
is a way for closed toes to be out
for summer citrus, to sunburn the desire
on such a long wavelength day
you arrived in rain,
you can't choose your name
one free blessing, and you're over
someday care of the mailer, return to sender
start by happening to be alive
now everything is real, even the world
when is there news like this?
oh it's nothing, it's nothing...
a sun judge at the trial,
called up for July duty
here it is, here we are,
map says we're lost,
interstate xyz

Epilogue

if I were to die
propose a solution—
make it good,
keep it close.
for example
tears all around
brisket in the sandwiches
speeches without words
prayers for the beach
claim an expense
save a little smile
bring a sudden song
make it only major:
a cloud progression for you
a seventh chord for me
your eyes for my face
give me your gaze
to be alone again,
like at Ta Prohm:
the two of us only
as myself,
I'm half the way there.

looking at the sun, running,
swimming with the sun, wet
is it the life or the death
that's the problem?
will you find it for me
complete a solution
so that all those left behind
will feel fulfilled

Notes

Notes

Notes

www.ingramcontent.com/pod-product-compliance
Lightning Source LLC
Chambersburg PA
CBHW021118080526
44587CB00010B/561